Series 644

the stories
of our
CHRISTMAS
CUSTOMS

by N. F. PEARSON
with illustrations by FRANK HAMPSON

Publishers : Wills & Hepworth Ltd. Loughborough

First published 1964   ©   *Printed in England*

Christmas Time

Every year in December we celebrate the birthday of Jesus Christ, by whose teachings all Christians try to live. That is why we call this time 'Christmas'—because we celebrate the 'Mass', or Church Service, for Christ. Sometimes, if we are lazy, we may write 'Xmas'. The 'X' stands for the Greek letter which, in Greece, is the first letter of Christ's name and frequently used there as a holy symbol.

At Christmas we remember that Christ taught us to love one another. We send cards, and give presents, to friends and relatives, and especially think of those less fortunate than ourselves. We watch and take part in Nativity Plays and Carol Services. We decorate our churches, chapels, schools and homes with green leaves, fir trees, paper decorations, candles and colourful electric lights. We eat and drink good things, and generally have a happy time.

Have you ever wondered why you hang up holly and not privet leaves, why you have good things to eat, and why it is that you get lots of presents even though it is not your birthday? This book will tell you why we do these things at Christmas.

4   *A Christmas scene in England*

7214 0189 9

Christmas Day

Jesus was born nearly two thousand years ago, long before accurate records were kept or birth certificates given. So nobody knows on which day He was born, nor whether He was born in the summer or in the winter.

Christians who lived a few hundred years after Jesus died, wisely chose the twenty-fifth of December to celebrate His birth, because this date was already a very special day. People did not work, but spent the day doing many of the things that we do now on Christmas Day.

Long before and long after Jesus was born, the twenty-fifth of December was the shortest day of the year. That is the day when there is less sunlight than on any other day. On the shortest day, people worshipped the sun and had special services where they prayed to the sun to come back and give them another summer. Christians knew that God made the sun and so they decided to worship the 'Son of God' on this day.

A different calendar is now used, and in it the shortest day falls on the twenty-first of December.

Primitive men worshipping the sun

The First Thousand Years of Christmas

The sun festivals were, in most places, occasions for generally having a good time. The Christians often took part in them, for although they did not believe in a sun god, they wanted to take part in the fun and joy. But these festivals were not always happy occasions, for in some places animals were sacrificed. In the year 601A.D. Pope Gregory ordered Christians to "no longer offer beasts to devils, but to worship God by feasting".

As more and more people became Christians, they thought of Jesus as a bringer of happiness, and so they thought of Him rather than of the sun at festival times. But this change of thinking took place very slowly.

In the fourth century, when the Romans adopted Christianity, they celebrated the birth of Christ with great processions to church on Christmas morning. The first we learn of Christmas in England was in 521A.D., when King Arthur went to York Minster to remember Christ's birthday, after he had won a great battle against the Saxons.

Christmas morning in Rome

The Second Thousand Years of Christmas

In the Middle Ages, Christmas was a very jolly time. Great feasts were held and the stern lords of the castles gave up their places to the 'Lords of Misrule', whose job it was to play jokes on people and keep everybody merry.

When Oliver Cromwell was Lord Protector of England, and there was no king, the Puritan Parliament made laws so that people would think of Christmas only as a solemn time. Fun and feasting were forbidden, because the Puritans said that such merrymaking had more to do with pagan sun worship than with Christ's birthday. They did not believe that people could worship God by having a 'good time'. To be fair to the Puritans, we must remember that people often behaved so badly at Christmas that they used the festival as an excuse to be hooligans.

You can imagine how much people hated the stern Puritan Christmas, and how great was the rejoicing when Charles II became king and allowed the old traditions again. The Scots disapproved of Charles II and kept to the Puritan ways. This is why Christmas in Scotland is not the festival that it is in England.

Medieval merrymaking.

Light, Heat and Candles

On the shortest day the pagan sun worshippers built fires which they thought would give the sun god strength to come back to life again. As the days lengthened they rejoiced because they knew the sun god had lived through the winter, and would bring them the light and heat of summer. So, long before Jesus lived, fire played an important part in worship.

Also, before Jesus was born, the Jews had a festival of lights in which candles were burnt. The festival was to remember the rebuilding of Solomon's Temple, and the candles were lit to show that truth was to be heard again in the Temple. The light of a flame has since this time been the emblem of truth. Christians have used the flame of the candle as a sign of the truth of Jesus, and you will notice that in many churches there are always candles on the altar.

There is a popular story that Martin Luther first put candles on a Christmas tree, to remind people of the stars that shone above Bethlehem on the night of Christ's birth. As naked flames are dangerous in the home, we to-day use coloured electric lights instead of candles.

Candle flame as the emblem of truth

The Crib

At Christmas time, in most schools and churches, children make a crib—that is, a group of statues showing all the people and animals who took part in the Nativity story. This is a custom which came from Italy and, like many Christmas customs, began even before Jesus was born. For at the Roman winter festivals, clay dolls were sold in the streets of Rome to be given as presents. When many Romans became Christians, they probably bought dolls which looked like Mary, Joseph, Jesus and other people of the Nativity story and so, in time, dolls were specially made to look like these people.

The most famous of cribs was that of St. Francis of Assisi, the good saint who was so kind to animals. He wanted people to understand how hard it was to live in a poor manger. He arranged to have a real live scene with people and a real ox and ass. This took place in northern Italy at Graecia in 1224 A.D,, and was followed by a service in which the Saint preached of the birth of a poor king.

Italian children making their crib

Nativity Plays

To-day, most of us look forward to two types of play at Christmas time—a serious Nativity Play, and a lighthearted pantomime or circus. These two types of entertainment show us how our Christmas is both serious and gay.

Throughout history, watching plays has always been popular at holiday or festival times. Before people could read, watching plays was one of the few ways of learning.

The people of the Middle Ages looked forward to watching plays made up from Bible stories. At first, these Miracle Plays, as they are called, were written by the priests and acted by their congregations. The Nativity stories in these early plays are very similar to the plays that are performed in most schools to-day before the Christmas holidays.

Later in the Middle Ages these Bible plays were performed by ordinary people in the town market places. These plays were acted on "pageants", which were large carts that could be drawn by horses from one place to another. As these plays were no longer played in church, they included amusing scenes which would have not been suitable in church.

Carols

A carol is a hymn which is full of joy and happiness. The word comes from the French 'carole', which was a dance, and long ago in England this word meant a dançe used to celebrate the shortest day of the year.

An early history book tells that about a hundred years after the death of Jesus, the Pope wanted people to sing in memory of the birth of Jesus. But the first Christmas hymns were not popular because they were sung in Latin, and only the priests could sing and understand them.

It was at St. Francis's Crib at Graecia, that carols were first sung in the language that ordinary folk could understand. The actors at Graecia composed carols to sing with the play. When the service was over, the singers strolled home singing, and so street carolling began.

This singing of carols, in words that could easily be understood, spread to other lands. In England, carols were sung by minstrels in the halls of the great lords, and later by street singers. And so to-day this tradition is carried on in house-to-house carolling by groups of children and church choirs.

Evergreens

Long before Jesus was born, evergreens played a special part in winter festivals. They decorated the homes and shrines of pagan peoples, not only because they were beautiful, but because their greenness showed that they were living when all other plants seemed dead.

In the cold northern countries, people hung evergreens in their homes for the spirits, or fairy people. They thought that the woodland spirits would live in the green foliage and, because it was warm inside, the spirits would not die of cold.

In the warmer land of Italy, Romans decorated their homes with evergreens. This was in honour of Saturn, god of all things that grew. At the time of the winter festival, evergreens were the only plants that seemed to be alive.

Mistletoe, holly and ivy had a special place in old pagan worship, for not only were they green, but they bore berries during the winter. Christians carried on decorating with evergreens, and they looked for Christian meanings in these plants.

Evergreens in winter

Holly

In Norway and Sweden the holly tree is known as the 'Christ-thorn' and its Danish name is 'Kristdorn'. At one time, the tree itself was used in the homes and churches of North Americans, and was called the 'holly' tree. It seems likely that the English word 'holly' may have come from the word 'holy'.

It is a 'holy' tree because it should remind us of the death of Jesus. The prickly leaves are like the thorns used in the Crown of Thorns that Jesus was forced to wear on Good Friday. The red berries are to remind us of the drops of blood that came when the thorns pierced His flesh.

Sometimes at Christmas time you will see a holly wreath fastened to a door or window. This is an old American custom. Americans living in our country have hung holly wreaths on their doors as they would do in America. Many British people have liked the idea, and copied it.

A holly wreath on a door: an old American custom

Mistletoe

There is a very old northern legend which explains why we hang up mistletoe at Christmas.

Balder, the sun god, was so fine and great that the other gods promised never to hurt him. They placed a spell on everything, to take care of him. Water would not drown him, nor could arrows, swords and poisons kill him. When the gods were laying their spells, they forgot the mistletoe. Now Loki, the god of evil, found this out, and made a sharp arrow out of a mistletoe branch. He put the arrow into the hands of the blind god Höder, and guided Höder's hand so that the arrow struck Balder. Balder was killed, but the other gods brought him back to life again, and the mistletoe promised never to hurt anyone again. This story made the mistletoe an emblem of love.

Jesus taught that we should love others as ourselves, so Christians kept the mistletoe as an emblem of love. To remember this teaching, they kissed under it, and so we have the tradition of kissing under the mistletoe.

The death of Balder

The Christmas Tree

There is an old German legend which tells us how a Spruce Fir became the first Christmas tree.

A very holy man who lived in the eighth century was sent from England to Germany to preach about Jesus. His name was St. Boniface. On a frosty night in December, he was walking in a wood when he came upon a group of people worshipping a pagan god. This was the night when offerings were made to the god, and they had met beneath an oak tree to offer a human sacrifice of a little boy. Just as they were leading him forward, the Saint rescued him. St. Boniface felled the great oak, and as it fell to the ground, it left behind a little fir tree that had been growing between its roots.

Then the Saint turned to the people and said, "From this night, that little tree shall be your holy emblem. It is the wood of peace, for your houses are built of it. It is the sign of eternal life, for its leaves are ever green. It points to Heaven, and shall henceforth be called the tree of the Christ-Child."

St. Boniface felling the great oak

Christmas Ornaments and Decorations

To-day we can make the places in which we live and work very beautiful with colourful streamers, and balls, bells, crackers, and snowmen cleverly made from paper. We can buy stars, angels, and hundreds of different ornaments made from all kinds of materials. This was not always so. At the old pagan festivals there were only evergreen decorations, and for hundreds of years Christians decorated only with evergreens.

When Italians first made their cribs, any coloured cloth or paper was used that would make the cribs more attractive. In a similar way, people decorating with evergreens added coloured ribbons and pictures. From this early use of these materials has gradually grown a great industry in decorations, from paper streamers to delicate glass ornaments.

It is only in the last hundred years or so that these decorations have been used to any great extent. This was partly because people left the countryside to live in towns. It was not always possible to go out and pick evergreens, and so coloured paper was sometimes used instead.

Gifts

At festival times ancient people used to give gifts. In Northern countries the gods Woden and Odin were believed to give special gifts. In the days when the Romans worshipped many gods and goddesses, they went at the winter festival to the grove of the Goddess Strenia, and cut down branches of the trees to give as presents. Later the Romans gave more expensive presents at their New Year festival. When they conquered other countries, they took with them many customs, and this giving of presents at New Year was one of these customs. This is why in most countries presents are not given on Christmas Day but on New Year's Day. These presents have really nothing to do with Christ's birthday.

It is only in English speaking and German speaking countries that present giving has been brought forward from New Year's day to Christmas Day. The people of these countries use their gifts to remember the gifts given by the wise men to Jesus.

Christmas gifts with colourful labels and wrappings

Christmas Cards

Unlike most traditions of Christmas, the habit of sending cards at Christmas time is only about a hundred years old. In the same way that the Christmas present took the place of the New Year gift, the Christmas card began to take the place of the New Year card.

New Year cards, although only containing word greetings for the New Year, often showed a picture of the baby Jesus. One of the first known is a beautiful design showing the baby Jesus on a cloud. This card was printed in 1467 A.D. and can be seen at the British Museum. It seems that New Year cards became popular with the discovery of the printing press. The pictures on these cards show that the senders were remembering the birth of Jesus, although the cards had no Christmas message.

The first cards with Christmas Greetings on them were not unlike Birthday cards with pictures of animals, flowers, children and summer scenes. It was not until 1900 A.D. that cards from Germany with holly, snow scenes and Nativity scenes became popular.

Santa Claus

Children of many European countries used to find presents left for them by the good Saint Nicholas. In North America the children of European settlers were left gifts by someone who was as kind as St. Nicholas. He was called Santa Claus.

St. Nicholas used to ride from Spain on a horse and put presents in clogs and wooden shoes. North American children believed that Santa Claus had to travel from the North Pole over much snow, and used a sledge and reindeer. Laced leather shoes could not easily be filled, and so American children hung up their stockings instead.

During the nineteenth century, Santa Claus gave presents to children all over the world, and not just to American children.

It was an American who first drew a picture of the Santa Claus that we see illustrated at Christmas time. He was a cartoonist called Thomas Nast, and he drew these pictures in a paper, the Harper's Weekly, in the years 1863 to 1866 A.D.

Christmas Food

Every country that celebrates Christmas has its own special Christmas fare, but in no country is there so much special preparation of food as in our own land. The Italians have a saying for when a person is very busy. They say that 'he has more to do than the ovens in England at Christmas'.

We have always eaten a great deal at Christmas, but now we eat little compared with the amount of food that was eaten in the castles and manor houses during the Middle Ages. Enormous feasts were prepared. These often began with a boar's head, richly decorated, being ceremoniously carried to the high table.

When the Puritans ruled our country, feasting was one of the customs they stopped. Parliament ordered that people 'fasted', not 'feasted', on Christmas Day. This, as you can imagine, was not at all popular, so when the country once more had a king, there was great rejoicing when feasting was again encouraged. But people never prepared quite as much as in the days before the Puritan Parliament. Nevertheless, we still eat well—often too well—at Christmas.

Christmas dinner in Tudor England

From Boar's Head to Turkey

In some homes pork has always been eaten as the main meat of the Christmas dinner. This is probably because in olden days, pigs were killed late in November, when they had grown fat on the acorns and other nuts which were the only food they could then find in the forests. By Christmas they were ready to be eaten, and the feast began with the head of the animal.

After the pork would come roast peacock. The bird was expertly cooked, and looked very fine with its tail and other feathers replaced for decoration.

Turkeys first came from America, and these birds were unknown in England before sailors returned from the New World. An Englishman, William Strickland, first brought the birds here in the first half of the sixteenth century, and by the end of that century turkeys were being served at table. Early in the seventeenth century they had replaced the peacock in the Christmas dinner.

A sailor brings home a turkey

Plum Pudding and Mince Pies

Plum pudding is so called because in days gone by prunes, which are dried plums, were used in the making of the Christmas pudding. To-day we use currants, raisins and sultanas instead of prunes, but the other ingredients—suet, breadcrumbs, eggs and spices—are the same as they always have been.

Mince pies were once called mutton pies, because finely chopped or minced mutton was one of the main ingredients. Like the plum pudding, the remaining ingredients were much the same as those we use to-day. Although we no longer use meat, we still add shredded suet, which is animal fat, in the making of both mince pies and plum puddings.

Mince pies used to be oval, or cradle shaped, and not round as they are to-day. One book tells us that this was to remind people of the manger in which Jesus was born, and that the pies were to be eaten quietly as people thought about the infant Jesus. This is possibly why people to-day make a silent wish when they take their first bite, and why others consider it unlucky to cut a mince pie.

Making plum puddings in Victorian England

Boxing Day

Boxing Day is really St. Stephen's Day. St. Stephen was the first to die for preaching about Jesus. Therefore he has the honour of having his day next to Christ's birthday.

In many churches to-day, you will see boxes in which to put money for poor people. Years ago, this was much more common than it is now, because there were many badly fed and poorly clothed people. In the Middle Ages the priests opened these boxes on St. Stephen's Day, and divided the money amongst the poor. St. Stephen's Day, therefore, became known as 'Boxing Day'.

Later, it became the custom for wealthy people to give their servants gifts on this day. These were usually money gifts given in small boxes and called 'Christmas boxes'. About a hundred years ago 'Christmas boxes' became what they are to-day—just money gifts without a box. These were given to anyone, such as the lamp-lighter and postman, who had served people during the year. To-day, Christmas boxes are usually given before Christmas.

Money gifts to the poor in the Middle Ages

Pantomimes, Plays and Circuses

Pantomimes have been the traditional entertainment of the British for over two hundred years. Although the Pantomime is a British custom, it had its beginnings in the eighteenth century with the dancing of French comic dancers from the Paris fairs. To make these dances more interesting, and to give the dancers a rest, stories were added. These stories nearly always were taken, as they are to-day, from fairy tales and nursery rhymes.

As the years passed each theatre tried to put on a grander show than the other theatres. To make their pantomimes grander, theatre managers encouraged more changes of scenery and costume, and more magnificent scenery and costume. Acts became more varied so that they could include items by popular singers, comedians, ventriloquists, conjurors and acrobats, until in the Pantomime to-day we even have entertainers doing their turns under water or on ice.

Circuses have always been popular at Christmas, and in recent years they have, perhaps, become even more popular than the Pantomime. Plays for children and plays from children's books are also popular, 'Peter Pan' and 'Toad of Toad Hall' being the most famous.

New Year's Eve

Although at New Year we are not celebrating the birth of Christ, New Year is so close to Christmas that we include it in our Christmas celebrations. We leave Christmas trees and decorations up for New Year and we eat and drink almost as much at New Year as we have done at Christmas. In fact, in Anglo-Saxon England, New Year's Day was the twenty-fifth of December.

New Year's Eve is the time when friends meet to welcome the coming year. In most countries it is celebrated much more than is Christmas. In Scotland, particularly, New Year's Eve, which the Scots call Hogmanay, is the most important festival of the year.

It is a world-wide custom for a man or boy to enter the house after midnight to wish all inside, "A Happy New Year". In Scotland, this person is called the 'first footer'. The first footer in some places must be dark, and in other places he must be fair. In most places he must not enter empty handed and it is considered lucky if he carries a small piece of coal. A woman first footer is thought to be unlucky.

'First-footing'

New Year's Day

New Year's Day has not always been the first of January. Thousands of years ago, the ancient Egyptian New Year was in the middle of June, when the River Nile overflowed its banks. Even to-day, the New Year of the Jews and Hindus is not when we celebrate it. In Christian countries New Year has been celebrated on many different days. When Pope Gregory XIII, in 1582 A.D., caused the making of the calendar which we use to-day, January 1st was made New Year's Day because it had been so in Ancient Rome.

In Ancient Rome this day was one given over to the worship of the god Janus, from which we get the name of the month. Janus was the god of beginnings and endings. He had two faces: one looked backward at the old year, and the other looked forward to what would happen in the coming year. This is how we all think at New Year.

Most people look back at their own mistakes and make New Year resolutions, in which they promise not to make the same mistakes again.

The Roman god, Janus

Twelfth Night

Twelfth Day is the last day of Christmas. Nowadays, it is the day on which we take down the decorations. Some people still celebrate with Twelfth Night parties. As its name tells us, it is the sixth of January—just twelve days after Christmas Day.

This day is the feast of the Epiphany, which is remembered as the day on which the wise men were guided by the star to the stable at Bethlehem. In northern France, children go out on Epiphany Eve to meet the three kings on the roadway.

In days of old, these twelve days were all spent in feasting, singing, dancing, playing games and watching actors. In some places Christmas went on being celebrated after Twelfth Night, but Twelfth Night was always, after Christmas Day itself, the most festive day of the Christmas season.

There always used to be a Twelfth Night cake, and it seems likely that since Twelfth Night is no longer of such importance, the cake is now eaten on Christmas Day as Christmas cake.

The three kings

Series 644